The Secrets of the Young and Rich

Retire Rich, Retire Young!

I0486130

By Richard Cowles

Introduction

I want to thank you and congratulate you for downloading the book, *"The Secrets of the Young and Rich: Retire Rich, Retire Young"*.

We all reach a certain age where we start to compare ourselves to other people our age. We see a co-25 year old driving a Porsche while we're still using our family's minivan. We see Facebook photos of our high school batch mates travelling the world while we live a routine of 8-5 jobs to get paid salaries just enough to pay off credit card bills. And then once in a while, we come across stories that leave us in awe; stories about the accomplishments of other people. We imagine and we wonder how to get there.

If you've been in these prickly positions in the past, then it's time for change. You have made the right decision by purchasing this book because I will now show you how it's done. You don't need to wait for retirement to be able to travel the world. Everything you want is within your reach, believe it or not!

Why I Wrote This Book

Money was a big problem for me and my family when I was growing up. My mom had to take 2 jobs because our dad left us. I would often spend afternoons with the old lady next to our apartment because my mom couldn't afford childcare. We would always be late for rent, bills and other needs. We were barely living a life and I could see my mother so tired of this process, but never complaining.

At the tender age of 8, I told myself that I would do everything within my power to give my mother and myself the life we deserve. My mom passed on having the opportunity to have a better education and to marry someone just so she could look after me. This was my main motivation for making money as early as I can so that my mom can enjoy her life before her retirement age.

I know that a lot of young people share the same sentiments as mine. And I have learned the formula for this kind of success based on my own experiences and the experiences of others and I believe that this knowledge should be shared. Hence, this book!

Why You Should Read This Book

You should read this book because you deserve a great life! Everybody deserves a great life and no matter how much you deny it, you will need money to live a great life.

Take a look at the situations listed below:

- Susan is unable to buy her children simple stuff such as new shoes and clothes because she lives from pay check to pay check. Whenever she receives her salary, she ends up paying the bills, the rent and all their necessities. What's worse is the fact that Susan is a single mom. She barely rests and has time for herself.
- Tim, an IT technician, has been working for one company for the past 8 years. Up until now, he still lives with his mother and is still short of cash for mortgage. He can't buy his own home because he does not make enough money to do so. He is skilled and very smart but nevertheless underpaid.
- Bea, an online contractor, has trouble in looking for a stable job. She cannot get a regular 8 to 5 job because she needs to take care of her mother who is very sick. This makes it very difficult for her to pursue her own dreams. She can't buy her dream car and dream house!

Do you see the similarity in the above mentioned scenarios? Susan, Tim and Bea are skilled, they are persevering and yet they don't get the life they deserve. Why? Because they do not put themselves in the right position in order to get hold of the right opportunities.

If you find yourself in the same circumstances as Susan, Tim and Bea, then you definitely need to read this book and learn how you can be rich at a young age.

Copyright

Disclaimer

The information provided in this book is designed to provide helpful information on the subjects discussed. This book is not meant to be used, nor should it be used, to diagnose or treat any medical condition. For diagnosis or treatment of any medical problem, consult your own physician. The publisher and author are not responsible for any specific health or allergy needs that may require medical supervision and are not liable for any damages or negative consequences from any treatment, action, application or preparation, to any person reading or following the information in this book. Any references included are provided for informational purposes only and do not constitute endorsement of any websites or other sources. Readers should be aware that any websites listed in this book may change.

Table of Contents

Chapter 1 Eliminating Clutter

This chapter presses to be the most important of all the steps that you need to take before you can cross the bridge to getting rich. Most of us do not really think of this when setting financial goals. In fact, we don't care about everything else that is going on around us when the truth is everything that is going on around us has everything to do with getting rich.

When I use the term 'clutter', I am talking about all factors that are present in our lives that can possibly hinder us from reaching our financial goals. I dedicated a whole chapter to this because I had so much clutter in my life! So to let you better understand, here is a brief outline of my life's clutter that I had to get rid off before choosing to be rich. I suggest you get rid of them as soon as possible.

Imagine a box that you want to fill with gold. You have to clean that box and rid it of all the dirt before you can fill it with precious items.

Unclear Priorities – this is one clutter that most young people share. There are lots of you who think that you know what you are doing and for what purposes you are doing them for but the truth is you've got it all mixed up. You juggle so many things and you think you have your priorities straight. But if you do, then why are you in the same financial situation that you are in today?

Setting your priorities isn't rocket science. There are three simple steps on how you can take control.

Step # 1: Be Aware of Your Time - time is gold. It is literally gold because how you spend your time translates to cash. Take a piece of paper right now and write down the 24 hours in a day, and write down what you do every hour. Are you being productive enough? Or are you just pretending to be productive. We complain on a daily basis on how busy we are yet this business does not really lead us anywhere, does it?

I was once a person full of excuses until I realized that I was not trying to convince anyone but myself. The day I met that awareness, I started to set my priorities straight.

Step # 2: Your Satisfaction – upon looking at how you spend your regular work day, can you completely say that you are satisfied with the things that you do? Do you create an effective schedule that really helps you with your objectives for each and every day? Does it cover all the important areas of your life? It's vital that it covers more than just your work life because being a workaholic doesn't directly translate to a great life. You can be rich, but are you happy? You should also spend an ample amount of time on your personal development and on other aspects such as relationships.

Step # 3: Set New Priorities – it's time to change your routine. To help you do this, you need to answer the following questions:

- What is the most important thing in your routine?
- What do you need to spend more time on?
- What do you need to spend less time on?
- What areas of your life need attention?

Build new priorities based on your answers to the aforementioned questions. Remember, the clock is ticking. If you stop, the world does not stop with you.

Emotional Baggage – Again, you would think that this has nothing to do with your strive for success but it has everything to do with it. As young people, we tend to become very emotional and we just simply can't let go of things that destroy us more than improve us. We've all had challenges in the past. We all have those people that we abhor because of what they have done to us but is there really any use to keeping grudges against these people? Some young people would say that keeping grudges is a great motivation. It pushes you to work harder. And though this may be true, the hatred you have for others and your past will just disable you. So just learn to let go.

Where's Your Focus – Another thing that you can do to eliminate clutter is to focus on one thing at a time. When we are young and exposed to many opportunities, it's very easy to lose focus from one thing and move to the other because we think we have a lot of time in our hands. The truth is, every time we waste time focusing on the wrong things, we lose a lot and other people get ahead.

Your age should not be an excuse. Every young and successful person decided that they want to be rich and they have also decided on how to do it. Once they figured out the means on how to carry out their plans to reach their dreams, they practiced focusing on one single thing at a time.

You should do the same. Let go of all other activities that you think are unnecessary in your life. Your love life and social life can wait. Too much of it will really let you lose focus. The same is true with so many majors you are taking.

Just focus on one degree. Eliminate learning about too many investments and just focus on what you really have passion for.

Reduce Your Circle of Friends – They say that as you grow older, your list of friends become shorter. By the time you are 25, you already know who's there for the long run and who's just there because of your similar social settings. If you don't, you should start to assess who your real friends are because some may just be taking your time without helping you grow.

Besides, do you really need too many friends? You only need a few, those who you can really have real conversations with and those that you help improve and improve you. If you are having trouble choosing which ones to keep, just keep this in mind: a friend is someone who you can be with with ease. You don't need to create much effort in order for you to have any kind of conversation and you don't have trouble looking for something to do that you both want because you're practically the same person.

Debt – being rich means your bank accounts states positive. You cannot do this unless you get rid of all your negatives. You are young and that probably means that you suffer from impulsive buys sometimes but that's not an excuse. Get a pair of scissors and cut all your credit cards and promise yourself that from now on, you won't acquire any debt.

At this age, you've probably seen the dreadful effects of debt to people. It does not only make them poor, it makes them liable for so many things. Sometimes, it even takes years before these people can be free f debt. You don't want to leave a life full of debt, believe me. If you are thinking of loaning a house or car, stop right there and think for a minute. You can buy all these without any interest if you become rich and afford to buy it with cash. So be patient and just wait.

Start with a Clean Slate

Everybody who's been through a rough life wishes to have a clean slate. They want to go back to the start so they can avoid creating the mistakes they have done. But we all know that it doesn't work that way. We can't turn back time.

The reason why people wish to go back to the start is because they can't accept the embarrassment and pain that they've received because of the wrong things they've done. But if you think of it, all those mistakes gave you lessons. In fact, if it weren't for these mistakes, you wouldn't be who you are today.

You don't need to go back to the start, you just need to accept that you've made mistakes just like everybody else because you are only human. Moreover, you need to stop making the same blunders over and over again. And that's how you can fully say that your life is out of clutter!

Chapter 2 What Motivates the Young and Rich

I've given you a brief insight of what my motivation was. Now I want to share with you a story regarding a person that I respect very well. I met him on a trip to the Philippines. I can't really publish his name but I can tell you about his story. He is currently the Dean of Law in one of the famous Law Schools in the Philippines. He is a well-known and highly paid lawyer now and rightfully so. He has his own house, cars, a family, he travels the world and has a lot of time to spend on his hobbies. But it wasn't always that way.

This person was once an orphan. He did not have any family. He lived with different people growing up. He would walk to school while holding his slippers in his hands just so it won't get worn out right away. When he went to high school, he was in the care of a priest. Every afternoon, he would clean the church as his job so that the church would send him to school. College came and he was at wits end on how he could attend college. He was sitting under a mango tree, reading, when a pastor came to him and asked him about his story. The pastor took him on his care seeing that he has potential and gave him a janitorial job so that he could go to college and law school.

In between this life were a lot of struggles. He would transfer from room to room because he couldn't pay rent. He was not able to enjoy his whole childhood. There were nights when he didn't eat. It was an ultimate sacrifice. And his life ahead was his motivation.

Looking at the Future

Whenever he felt like giving up, he would close his eyes and imagine how it would be if he could overcome all of this. Once he would, he could go right back on track and focus despite all the pains he went through.

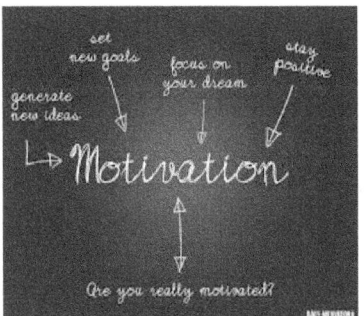

Looking at the future is a great way on how you can stay motivated. Let me help you out on this one. Take a piece of paper and write down your answer to the following questions:

• What kind of house would you like to have? Describe it very well, to the detail. If possible you can go ahead and draw it.

• Where do you want to travel? Be specific with the places. Research on activities that you can do on those places as well.

• What business would you like to put up? Go ahead and write down a name for your business and a short description.

- How many kids do you want? Write down names for them as well. Describe where you want them to go to school, what extracurricular activities you want them to learn and the like.
- What car would you like to drive? Describe the color, type and even the accessories you even want to add.
- What charities would you like to help? Describe your beneficiaries and why you chose this charity.

It's such a joy to answer those questions isn't it? Did you notice that I want you to answer in detail? Here's the reason why.

You need to look into the future with a clear vision. You cannot simply say "I want to be rich" or "I don't want to be able to send my children to school". You need to be specific about everything: the walls of your home, the color of your car, the skills you teach your children, the people you help and the like. Envisioning in detail makes it easier for you to stay motivated. Believe me, this works!

Your "Whys"

Your "whys" are basically the questions you ask yourself. These are the self-doubts that you don't really need clarification to but are great motivators. For example, one of my greatest "whys" is "Why was I given a very tough childhood?" Asking myself this question makes me realize that the childhood I had molded me to be the strong and skilled person that I am today. Without that kind of childhood, I would not have learned how to be diligent in everything I do. Whatever questions you may have about your existence will further lead you to figuring out how you can use it as a motivation.

The Magic of the Vision Board

The Vision Board is a popular concept made popular by many motivation experts all over the world. Basically, it is a board of pictures or words that represent our goals. When you look at it often, you will get reminded of your goals and you will stay motivated. The vision of your dreams will empower you to work harder and to never stop trying to reach your aspirations in life.

The million dollar question is: Are vision boards effective? YES THEY ARE! Every successful person I know now, and probably every person successful person you know as well, has had a vision of where they are today. Moreover, they have put this vision in paper and looked at it on a regular basis to stay encouraged.

The reason why the vision board is very effective is because one of the most helpful mind exercises that you can do is to visualize. If you're familiar with the book *"The Secret"*, it comprehensively explains how to vision boards helps you stay enthusiastic in all your daily endeavors. The best-selling book explains that when you visualize, you emit a very powerful frequency to the Universe that dramatically aids in making your visualizations come true. Whether you think you can or you can't, it's up to you. BELIEVE IT OR NOT, IT'S ALL IN THE MIND!

Olympic athletes have been using this strategy for years so they can improve their performance. They visualize that they arrive at the finish line first against all the other competitors and it happens. Psychology Today wrote a report regarding the comparison of real life weights to visions. When you carry weights, you develop your muscles. It's the same thing when you visualize, you also develop your future.

So how do you create a vision board that works? Is this really all about what you want? Actually, it's much more than what you want to happen, it should also include how you want to feel. For example, if you put a photo of your dream car in there, you should also insert a photo of you inside the car, because this will remind you of how good it feels to be driving your own hard owned automobile.

Add in there things that remind you of how far you've come as well because it symbolizes that you are steps closer to your vision. I pin my certificates to my vision boards or trinkets such as the very first dollar I ever made from my own business. If you have friends or other loved ones who send you handwritten notes of encouragement, fuse that into your vision board as well.

There are no rules in creating your vision board! Go all out! It doesn't matter if it's big or several small ones. It doesn't matter if it's pretty or not. What matters is what's in it and the fact that it's something that you want to happen in your life. Go ahead and make one for you today. Place it somewhere where you often see it like your office, refrigerator, kitchen cupboard and the like.

Overcoming Obstacles

The obstacles you have overcome will keep you motivated because they remind you that you are strong.

The road to richness is not smooth. You will go through many obstacles such as failures, haters, wrong decision and the like. What sets apart a successful young man from someone who isn't is how they handle these obstacles.

One trick that you can use so you can stay on track is taking a trip down memory lane. Remember where you came from and where you are today. It may not be where you want to be exactly, but you are a step closer. It means that you have come far from where you were before. Remind yourself of your first crappy apartment, the old car that wouldn't start during winter, the landlady who would embarrass you when you couldn't pay rent, the food you ate because you couldn't afford much, the dozens of promissory notes you had to write to your school administration because you did not have enough money for your tuition fee and all those moments when you felt like giving up, but you didn't. You didn't give up before, so don't give up now.

Chapter 3 Delayed Gratification

THIS IS A VERY IMPORTANT CHAPTER OF THIS BOOK. Usually, books about getting rich and becoming successful would just put the concept of delayed gratification under a chapter. However, in this particular book I'm writing addressed to the youth, it's vital that you, the reader, see the need of delayed gratification in your life today. Many young people, some I've seen firsthand, fail in their endeavors because they don't practice this principle.

What is Delayed Gratification?

Delayed gratification is the general setback of giving yourself the things you want for the time being so that you can better gratify yourself in the future.

The Youth and Delayed Gratification

The problem with the youth is that they have a one day millionaire mindset. This is most especially true for people who are experiencing, for the first time, how to make money with their own efforts. Once they get their first pay, they would immediately buy themselves things or go party. This happens even more when the youth works with other youth. It's a whole group of workers that do not know how to delay their gratification.

Spending Right

Do not satisfy your impulses with money. You will feel good for a while but you very well know that you will regret it later. You are blinded by new gadgets released in the market, you want to splurge for a night out with friends, you want a new car even if your old one is still working – all of these are normal and human wants but they are not needs. You need to resist and learn to say NO to your impulses even if you are compelled by society or your peers.

Delay giving yourself all these things so you can save more, invest more and profit more for better things in the future. Starting today promise yourself to do the following:

- Do not buy anything that you don't need.
- Don't buy something to replace something unless it is already completely destroyed or impossible to repair.
- Delay travelling to near places so that you can save up to travel to farther places.
- Say no to vices such as drinking, smoking and gambling.
- Don't be influences by print media and the society. Remember that everything you see in magazines and in the television are over-exaggerated, grandeur but unnecessary lifestyles of people.

In short, DON'T SPEND THE MONEY YOU DON'T HAVE TO BUY THE THINGS YOU DON'T NEED TO IMPRESS THE PEOPLE THAT YOU DON'T LIKE.

Strategies on Delayed Gratification

Strategy 1: Know Your Values

Know what is really important to you. Don't do something right now that is less important just because it is easier to acquire. Wait for the right time and practice the values that you really believe in. Don't be the type of person who gives in right away. Learn the value of patience, especially with money.

Strategy 2: Be Clear with Your Goals

If you are not clear with your goals, it's going to be difficult for you to delay gratification. For example, if you want to buy the iPhone6 but only have money for the iPhone5, don't buy the latter. Wait until you have the money for the former because it's going to me more gratifying since that was your original goal.

Strategy 3: Create a Plan

A plan that you have created on your own will help you in staying focus. It will aid in maintaining your means of delaying your gratification. If you continue to look at the bigger prize, it will be a breeze for you to say 'No' to the smaller prizes along the way.

Strategy 4: Prioritize

Do not dare spend anything on something that isn't your priority! This is a strategy that the youth needs to master. For example, everybody's need is to put food on the table. But some kind of spend too much because of eating out. I mean, do you really to dine out? It's even a lot healthier if you prepare food at home, cheaper, too!

Strategy 5: Reward Yourself

It's okay to reward yourself from time to time especially if you deserve it, remember, ONLY WHEN YOU DESERVE IT. If you achieve something, get yourself a little reward to compensate for your hard work. Make sure that this compensation is equal to the amount of work that you do. Don't reward yourself with a road trip to somewhere far for a simple achievement. Reserve travelling for bigger achievements.

Chapter 4 What is Money?

You need to manage your description of money so that you know how you can make it grow. Some just see it as a form of currency. These people who have this kind of description of money just live from pay check to pay check. You should see money as something powerful, something that can dramatically change your life.

Is Money Really Evil?

You've probably heard this quote many times in the past. People say that money is the root of all evil because many people do the most absurd and appalling actions just to get hold of money. Though that may be true, it has nothing to do with money. The source of evil is not money, the source of evil is man itself.

In fact, on the contrary, money can be a source of good evil. Bo Sanchez, a famous pastor-entrepreneur, told a story in one of his books that during his times in the church as a young man, he came across a poor person who was asking for his help. Even though he had the heart to help, he didn't have the money. That's when he realized that if he wanted to do good for the people, he will need money to do so. And that was his main motivation in getting rich.

It's all in how you use your money. If you use it for evil, that doesn't make money evil, it just makes you evil. If you use it for good, then you are good. Money is subject to how you utilize it. This is why it's important to note that whatever endeavors you enter, you have to make sure that they are 100% good, that they do not violate any laws of your country or any general laws of man. At first it seems like doing it the wrong way is the fastest way to make money but let me tell you that it is also the fastest way to lose it.

Money and Logic

Poor people don't see money logically. Instead of using logic, they use their emotions with handling money thus, it ceases to exist very fast. Don't spend just because you feel like it. Emotional spending is the worst kind of spending. A rich person would see money as "what it is" and "what it's not"; no more, no less. If you think of money logically, it will open you to opportunities that can logically create money as well.

Money Is What Keeps You Alive

This is the primary thing that you need to keep in mind. Whether you like it or not, money makes the world go round. You cannot move without it. You need money so you can function as useful part of the society. You can't be a good dad without money, you can't be a good son without money, you can't upgrade your business to franchises without money. YOU NEED MONEY and that should be enough motivation.

Chapter 5 Overcome Your Anxiety and Improve Your Confidence

What separates the successful from those who are not despite their young age is the fact that they are confident and not anxious about anything at all. Anxiety and low self-confidence are two things that will internally destroy you. I say this because I have seen it in many people I know. Truth is, you've probably seen this in many people as well. This chapter does not only teach you how to conquer your anxiety and improve your confidence, it also shows you what to do and what not to do in order to succeed. I hope that you really take all the information in this chapter by heart because it will help you not only in making money but also in your daily social relations to the world.

Worrying Too Much

The reason why we worry too much is because we fear failure. In a world where most rich people are in their late adulthood stage, it's normal for young people like us to feel very worried about every decision we make but the truth is WORRY WORKS ON US, IT DOESN'T WORK ON US.

Constant worrying takes a heavy toll on us physically, mentally, spiritually and emotionally. It can leave us sleepless every night but won't help the results that we anticipate in the future.

The reason why we worry is because we think that doing so may help us find a solution or that we don't want to be surprised with the results we get. But it's only giving you a hard time. You have to cut the habit of worrying today because it affects your productivity a lot.

If you want to get rid of worrying, you need to think of this simple philosophy: IF A PROBLEM IS SOLVABLE, THEN GO AHEAD AND THINK OF A SOLUTION BUT IF A PROBLEM HAS NOT SOLUTIONS THEN THERE'S NO USE WORRYING ABOUT IT.

Being Whole Hearted with a Venture

When you enter a business venture, it's highly important that you know what you are doing. Otherwise, you will be half-hearted about it and if you are, chances are, it's really not going to work out.

Decide that you want to succeed. This is the only way for you to become whole hearted in your daily undertakings. If you don't believe in the gamble you are about to enter, chances are you will lose. And if you've been battling in the business scene for quite some time, you know that every new business venture is a gamble, you might lose and you might win. Either way, you have to trust your instincts and skills.

Taking Risks

There are many instances when you are required to take risks as an adult. Often times, when it's your first time to get yourself into something, you'd often think that you are just getting yourself into trouble. Until you realize that it could have been a great opportunity for you.

Risks are a part of life. And if there's one thing that all the young and successful people share, it's the fact that they all took a risk. They were once scared and they thought a lot of times before investing on something but they still did because they were brave enough to do so.

As a young adult, you should also have this kind of confidence. It's important that you believe in yourself and in your decision making skills. Otherwise, you will end up investing in the wrong business ventures.

Building Your Self-Confidence While You Are Young

If you're young and want to get rich, you will need to talk to many people on a daily basis. Building relationships and rapport is an indispensible part of getting rich. If you don't have the self-confidence of an experienced CEO, then you are going to get eaten in just about any industry you join.

IT'S TIME TO GET FIERCE! Forget about all the childhood problems that caused your low self-esteem, take a step back from all the people who pressure you to look or act in a specific way, just forget about the outside world for a moment and channel your inner spirit.

The very first thing you need to do in order for you to gain the self-confidence to be yourself. If you try to be someone else, you're going to live a very frustrating life. Get in the habit of pleasing yourself instead of pleasing someone else. Starting today, be in charge of your own happiness.

Next, it's time to change your mental diet. Only listen to what builds you and screen out everything else that pulls you down. This may be difficult to do when even your own family does not believe in your skills but it's no reason to feel less confident about yourself. Don't focus on negativity even if the whole world seems to go against your goals. Just keep on going.

Third, you need to stop comparing yourself to others. The only person that you need to be better than is the person you were yesterday. Don't let other people be your benchmark. Their success is different from yours and you should never pressure yourself to be like them.

Fourth, keep in mind that it's up to you to keep positive affirmations about yourself. Get rid of your need for self-recognition and stop looking for affirmations from other people. What's important is how you see yourself.

Fifth, develop yourself. Make a Version 2.0 of who you are, a more improved one and an individual who is ready to take on any challenge there is! If you don't make positive changes like this, you will remain to be the poor person you know. If you reinvent yourself, then you might just be the perfect person to handle billions of dollars.

While developing the aforementioned, be free from doubt about your assessment of yourself. If you are in denial of your insecurities, then you will never get rid of them. Take a look at your weak points. Personally, I was very insecure about the way I looked when I was 18. I didn't have the money to buy nice clothes and I didn't look so snappy. That's why when I started working, I made sure to do something about it. I thought "how can people believe my investments and offers if I don't look believable.

The same should go for you. Be a person free of insecurities. Once all insecurities are gone, that's the time that your real self-confidence will emit and people will feel how truly confident and unquestionable your personality is.

Chapter 6 What Rich People Do Differently

There are thousands upon thousands of industries in the world. Your skill set will surely fit somewhere. You've probably searched online and offline on ways on how you can generate money and you have come across stuff that you've tried and you're still willing to try. The question is - are you looking in the right places?

Any employer who is looking to hire an employee will tell you that they compensate well when in fact, they just pay you the average. If that is their definition of "good compensation" it doesn't mean that it also needs to be your definition as well.

Starting from the bottom is a must. No one starts on top right away unless they are children of rich people handed a silver platter every now and then. If you are just like me, then it's possible to go from rags to riches. However, it doesn't necessarily mean that the climb towards the top should be slow. There are many ways on how to get rich quick. Here is a guide on how you can make LOTS of money!

Rich People Make Use of Their Time Wisely

Poor people are so because they procrastinate too much. They don't make use of their time wisely. Sadly, in addition to this, whenever they procrastinate, they make excuses such as being tired, being too busy and so and so when in fact, they can still be productive. I pity this people because whenever they make excuses, they don't really try to convince anyone else, they just convince themselves.

You have to plan your day from the moment you wake up until you fall asleep at night. Do this before the next day begins. Don't check your email. Nothing urgent is in there. If it's urgent, people will call you. Just start working and check your email once you are free. Make it a goal to be productive every day. One lazy moment can lead to a lazy day and one lazy day can lead to a streak of a lazy week. Fight indolence and keep on working.

Rich People Build Useful Networks

You need to know people so you can make lots of money. This isn't being about befriending every business tycoon you meet. Friendship is not the question here. Having a network means that you know people for the right purposes so when you need their services, you can immediately contact them.

I have a cousin who opened up a business somewhere in California that required a big network. She wanted to be a party planner. At first, I was a bit hesitant in helping her out with the idea because California was considered a party central and a lot of party planners are already in the area. People would book weddings, anniversaries, proms and the like in this area and if you are a popular party planner, you would really make a lot of money. However, she wasn't.

She explained to me that we had a big chance at profiting from her planning skills. I had no questions about her skills, basing from our past family parties that she planned, she is indeed a commendable one! I was more in question of her target market and how she can be competitive in this industry when there are so many party planners in California.

So I was doubtful at first until she showed me a list of the network she has been building for the past year. She really was into this business! The list contained numbers and contracts with florists, tailors, caterers, candle manufacturers and the like. She talked to every one of them and got great deals for every need. She has a discount with the florist, the wedding gown maker, the photographer, it was just unbelievable what she had pulled off!

You should create a network that is beneficial for you as well. Note that my cousin made sure that her contacts were also benefited. She gives free advertising for these contacts and she makes sure that they still make money despite the discounts and deals she signed up for.

Always make it a win-win situation for you and your network.

Rich People Have a To-Do List

In line with making use of your time wisely, if you want to be rich, you have to practice making a to-do list on a daily basis. A poor person would just "Go with the FLOW" so as many youngsters do today. Rich people, on the other hand, have a schedule they follow.

Making a schedule is the easy part, sticking to it is the more challenging. You have to STRICTLY follow your to-do list. If it says you have to get up by 6 AM, then you get up by 6 AM. If it says no open slots for coffee with friends, then you're going to have to get a rain check for every coffee date. If you stick to your goals for the day, it will be easier for you to build up your wealth.

Rich People are Healthy

Rich people know the ill-effects of living an unhealthy lifestyle. They count calories, they get the exercise they need and they don't waste money on vices. They know how important it is to stay healthy and how expensive it is to be sick.

Seriously though, healthcare provided for by the government is so scarce in so many areas in the world that's why rich people do everything they can take care of their well-being.

Just take a look at Steve Jobs. He was a very rich man, but he was not able to use all of his money to cure pancreatic cancer. He could have done more great things if he had taken care of his health. Even his billions couldn't get him out of this predicament.

Rich people know that money can't buy health, so they need to work hard to maintain it.

Rich People Read at least 30 Minutes a Day

Reading is a habit that all rich people share. Note that this reading is not for recreational purposes. They read material that would help them widen their knowledge in their field. They admit that they still lack some of the skills they need so they work on getting to the point of perfection every day.

If you have a smart phone or tablet, it's very easy to do this on a daily basis. Read at least one article a day about your field in the internet. Be aware of the new trends in the market. I like to keep bookmarks of websites that are related to the stock market and different pages that have constant updates regarding sales and marketing. I like subscribing to these pages because they update me on what's going on.

Knowledge is easily acquired today because of the presence of technology. Therefore, there's no reason for you not to read because you no longer need to go to the library or enroll a course just to learn.

Rich People are Particular with Time Periods

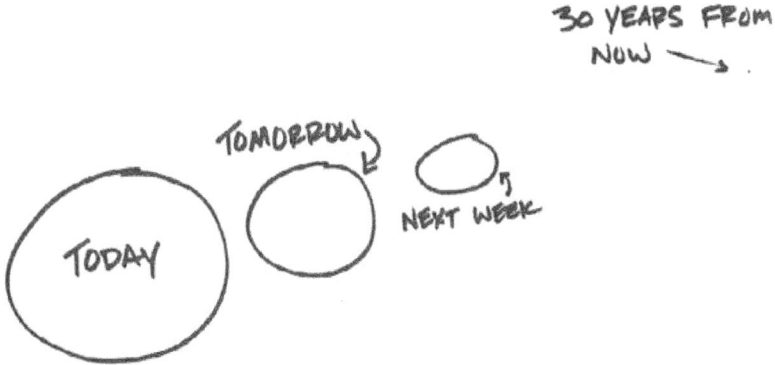

When a rich person plans, he does not only take into consideration his plan for the next day. He looks beyond tomorrow. He has a to-do list for everyday. And then he has a plan for the next week. He has set goals for the month, for the year and even for the decade.

Looking into the future and writing down a very specific timeline will help you get rich. You should have short-term, medium-term and long-term goals. All of the three should be posted somewhere where you can always see them so you get constantly reminded of the truly important tasks that you need to carry out so you can make your dreams come true.

True enough, rich people do indeed have a different way of doing things. In fact, if in your lifetime you have been exposed to both poor and rich people, you can easily decipher one from the other because a rich man would be humble, diligent and quiet while a poor person has so many things to say without any information to back it up and is full of excuses.

Ask yourself, are you the poor man or are you the rich man? If you are the poor man, it's not yet too late to make changes that will dramatically improve your life!

Bonus Chapter How Rich People Think

Rich people are rich because they think differently compared to the average person. If you don't earn as much as you want and if you are living from pay check to pay check and if you are in so much debt, then it's time to change your thinking. A lot of us in the world are hard working. Sometimes, a hard working person can even do more work compared to a rich person but still does not get the financial freedom he deserves. This is because it's not just in the way you work, it's more on the way you think.

Live your life on the following thoughts and you will surely become rich.

Thought # 1: Poverty is the Root of all Evil

As mentioned in Chapter 4, money is not the root of all evil. Rather, the lack of money is. Admit it. Many issues all over the world stem from lack of money. There is a higher rate of crimes such as theft, robbery, murder and the like in areas that are really poor. I'm not being judgmental here. I am merely stating facts.

Take a look at couples who get divorced or annulled. One of the top reasons why marriages fail is because partners also fail to provide the needs for the family. Either the wife leaves the husband because the husband is not rich enough or the husband leaves the wife because she can't work because she needs to take care of the kids. Speaking of kids, children also go into drugs, premarital sex and other lascivious and dangerous activities because parents fail to give them the time and attention they need because they are busy making ends meet.

Stop being brainwashed about how money can make you evil. Money will enable you to help people. Lack of money will potentially make you bad.

Thought # 2: Rich People Move

Poor people have the lottery mentality while rich people move. If you really want to be rich, you have to stop waiting for luck. The average person would wait for God's grace, her husband's promotion, his boss' raise and so many more. People really need to stop relying on other people for their future. Move for yourself and move on your own.

Thought # 3: Selfishness is a Virtue

We all want to be altruistic. It's a good value that the human race shares. But if you are out there just trying to save the world, then you won't be able to save yourself. Being the superhero is such a middle class problem. You look for something to be proud about when you can focus on making yourself better. Be a little bit selfish. It could go a long way when you try to ignore the problems of others while you focus on your own problems first. When you've gained that solid kind of income that you've dreamed of, then that's the time that you should start helping.

Thought # 4: Acquire Specific Knowledge

Jack of all trades but a master of none, are you? Then you're in a lot of trouble. Once you reach the age of 20, you should already know what type of knowledge you want to be an expert in so you can concentrate on that. If you keep on jumping from one career to the other, chances are, you are going to end up not being able to find one job or source of income that you want.

You have to decide what you want to be and you need to be the best in it. If you have the money, get an education. Enrol lessons that will widen your knowledge and that will equip you with the skills you need in order to be the best in the field you choose.

Thought # 5: Challenges Will Make You Better

Rich people are always up for the challenge. An average person would say something like "I won't expect anything so I won't get disappointed". A rich person, on the other hand, would say "Bring it on! What doesn't kill me makes me stronger!" Can you imagine if we lived in a world where everybody shares the same mentally as the latter? Oh, that would just be awesome!

You have to raise your expectations of yourself so you can, too, be better. If you should aim then aim high. There are no limits to your goals, just your imagination.

Thought # 6: You Have to Work on Being Someone

Whether you like it or not, not everybody can be rich. If you are not SOMEONE, then you can't get the wealth you dream of. While the masses are fixated on doing the mediocre, regular, day to day stuff, you should be concentrating on being extraordinary. This refers back to thought # 4 where you have to enter a specific expertise. Don't be boring, be a risk-taker!

Thought # 7: Surround Yourself with Like Minded People

Once you know what your thoughts should be, you have to be careful with choosing the people you hang out with. It's significant that you spend time with people who have the same thoughts so you don't pull each other down. On the contrary, you help each other strengthen your high points and eliminate your weaknesses.

The first step to getting young and rich is to change your thoughts. If your mindset is still stuck on being an average person, then you're not getting anywhere. Move away from the conventional thinking of people your age and think like a billionaire. Once you do, that is where all the magic will begin.

Conclusion

The stereotype for rich people would usually show us a picture of a man in a suit in his late 40's. You don't need to be part of this stereotype. You don't need to work in a corporation for so many years before you can say that you are rich. It's time to turn the tables and to show the world that even young people like YOU are capable of living a secured and worry-free life. Question is – are you ready?

As I look back to the last 20 years of my life, I would be able to categorize the first 10 and the last 10 differently.

The first 10 was terribly difficult. I literally had nothing and I was starting from scratch. All I had was my skills and my perseverance to look for the right places to use them for. My goals then were quite simple: to be able to put food on the table and to make sure that we don't get kicked out from the small apartment that me and my mom was renting.

The last 10 years was when my life started to really change. I paid my dues heavily during the first 10 years that's why I really got what I deserved in the next 10.

Moral of the Story: Life will get really tough and your journey ahead will have lots of problems that you will feel like giving up. But that is no reason to do so. You have to stay focused even if you feel so beaten up. When everything is put in the right place, you will find that everything that happened to you has a purpose and that every battle you've ever won leads to something great.

Are you ready to be a rich young man or a rich young woman? Are you prepared to take over your life and finally be able to live it to the fullest? YOU NEED TO BE READY! Because now that you've read this book, you already have the power to do so.

One Last Thing...

If you enjoyed this book or found it useful I'd be very grateful if you'd post a short review on Amazon. Your support really does make a difference and I read all the reviews personally so I can get your feedback and make this book even better.

If you'd like to leave a review then all you need to do is click the review link on this book's page

www.ingramcontent.com/pod-product-compliance
Lightning Source LLC
Chambersburg PA
CBHW070759180526
45168CB00004B/1684